Early Life Narratives:

Venetian, Ionian, British and Spartan Origins

by Joan Markessini

DORRANCE
PUBLISHING CO
EST. 1920
PITTSBURGH, PENNSYLVANIA 15238

Dorrance Publishing Co
585 Alpha Drive
Suite 103
Pittsburgh, PA 15238

Visit our website at www.dorrancebookstore.com

ISBN: 978-1-6491-3362-5
eISBN: 978-1-6491-3591-9

Contents

To My Parents and Theirs,

Atlantic's roiling waters, past

    Their lives they held— high and fast.

    Dared the odds; faced what came.

    To find the Country that would transfigure their lives:

Or steal them.

List of Illustrations

Prologue

I am the only daughter of Mediterranean European immigrants to the United States of America; those immigrants, my parents, were born into prosperous families during the first quarter of the twentieth century. Both experienced warfare directly as young adults in their late teens.

I am also a twin sister to an only brother, born in the Borough of Manhattan, New York City during a World War. In a time when one or the other of twins, if not the mother as well, died during childbirth, Dimitri and I both struggled to survive it. He became an engineer and I, a doctor.

These are the stories of my parents, their births, arrivals, survivals, and marriage and of their parents before them: Markessini, Likouthi, Vlahos, Govostes.

My parents and theirs enjoyed marriages of more than fifty years. Dimitri and I benefited from their sustained love of one another and of us.

Joan Markessini

These narratives—of Venice, its Ionian Kingdom, Great Britain and its Empire, and Sparta, Greece—are like shards from a fine Venetian mirror held up to conjoined memories

I. A Given Name

My Mother's given name was Diamond, odd considering her colloquially used name here in this country—Diana. She was baptized Diamanto (in Greek), the name her immediate family and other relatives used including my father. Perhaps my Grandmother (baptized Vasilike, "Queen" in English) saw her infant daughter that way because she was herself a teenager, still hardly more than a child when she gave birth to her first baby girl. Especially when her pregnancy was so anguished; her baby was born two months premature in a lonely bed in a hospital room in Sparta, Greece. She had arrived there underweight and exhausted.

Knowing she was in trouble, she had fled the small clan village of Vresthina where she had been visiting relatives and sought the help she knew she could not get from the midwives of the village. I have been to those mountains of my Grandmother's village. They are harsh and made of shale. In winter, at that time, the only way down from their heights to the sea had to be by ox cart.

My Grandmother confided to me when I was still a child, how fearful she had been of the midwifery practices she had seen and heard of there. As much as has been written positively about the place of midwives in perinatal healthcare; at the turn of the century in rural Mediterranean Europe, she wanted none of it.

Before she left home in Boston to venture into the surrounds of Sparta, Vasilike already knew about the hospital in Sparta. It had been built with the financing and under the auspices of a physician born in Sparta who had arrived in Boston at age ten, graduated Harvard Medical School, practiced in the United States, and retired to help his countrymen in the region of his birth. My Grandfather, John, had asked his young wife to look up this man and entrusted her to make a contribution to his work on their behalf, little knowing that his request would enable her survival and that of their unborn child. It was he, now Director of the Hospital, who had personally assumed the care and recovery of mother and child.

She stayed there alone mostly lying in bed on doctor's orders for two full months until she and her "Diamond" were strong enough to survive the long voyage back to Boston harbor and home. It was a miracle that both young mother and premature infant survived. (The good doctor quite possibly recognized the signs of toxemia and almost certainly saved her life.)

My Grandfather would not let her go alone again overseas, although that time he had given in to her desperate pleadings and longing for home and

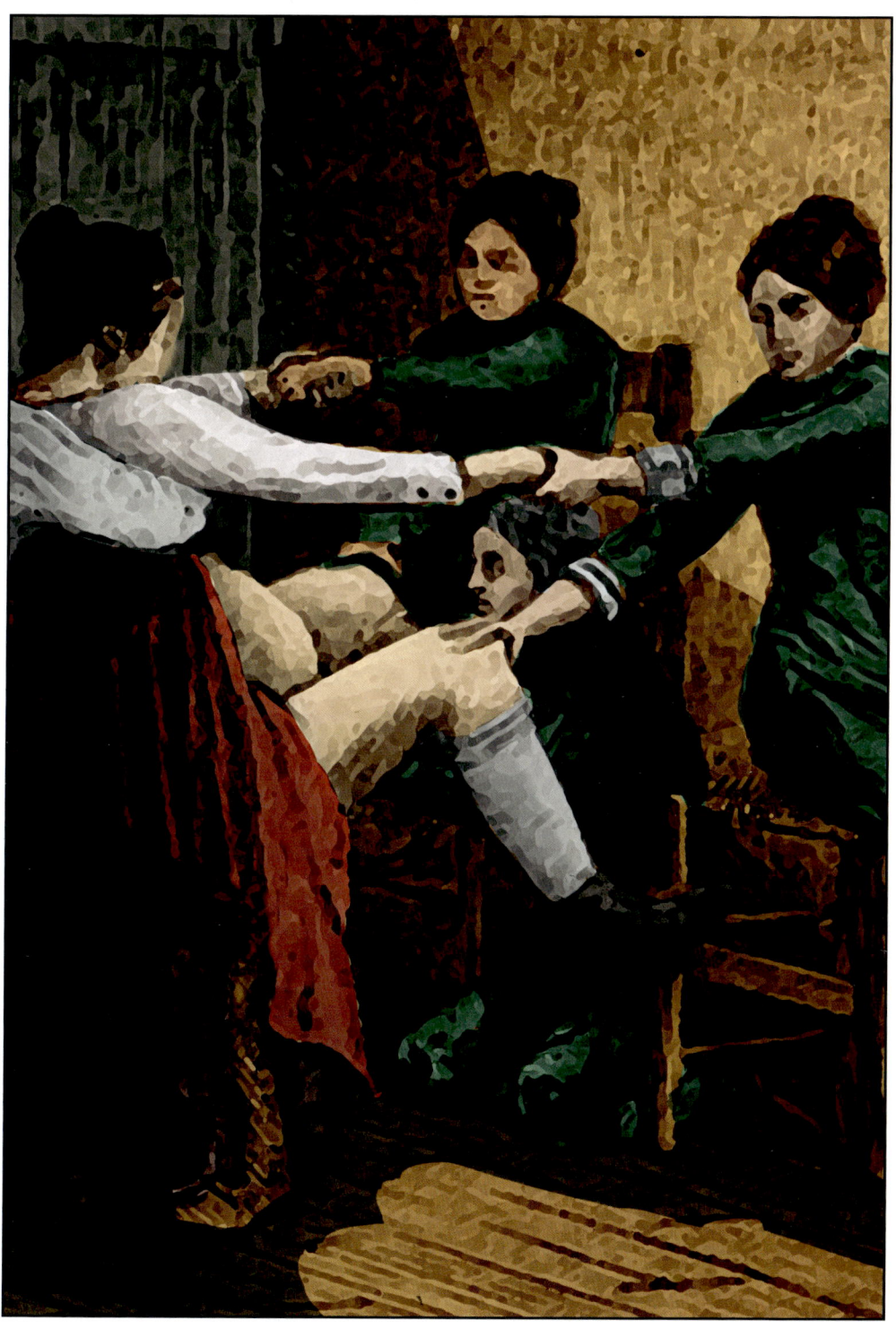

Mid-wives Attend a Young Mother Giving Birth-Europe.

for her Mother there. Perhaps he felt sorry for her and relented; she was so much younger than he and a bride at sixteen in an arranged marriage that he had yearned for (because, he told me, she was so beautiful) but to which she had only quietly acquiesced at the urging of her protector in America, her father's brother. From the time she bore him a healthy son, their first child, she had suffered three miscarriages, perhaps all three resulting from toxemia. Hard to bear physically and emotionally. She may have pleaded for her survival; she may have already suspected she was pregnant. He let her go.

Mother was naturalized at some point after her arrival in the United States; by then both Grandfather and Grandmother had become citizens. Once that piece of family history became known to us, my twin Jamie (Dimitri in Greek) and I were able to realize that we are children of immigrants, both Mother and Father.

But of her two first names, I think my Mother liked it best when she heard my father call her as he always did by her name Adamantia,* a variation of Diamanto. It was the name her Mother also used. In any case, for my part, I liked her American-English name, Diana, but also as such, if not more, her given name Diamanto. How my Grandmother came up with that particular substitute, Diana, for her baby girl's name I will never know; I did not think to ask her. Except the opening three syllables sound like those of Diamanto or she just may have sensed my Mother's strong and questing spirit.

In the histories of these maternal grandparents and their firstborn daughter lies the truth of how difficult survival and transitions were for them and other immigrants like them, the kind of parallel foreground/background existences they felt they had to lead. These dual existences such naming practices reveal may not be uncommon—the one presented to the broader cultural world of the newly arrived; the other hidden in the culture of origin.

<u>Note:</u>* Adamantia, "Diamond" (Αδαμαντία) derives from the Ancient Greek word adámas (ἀδάμας), meaning "strength, invincible, unbreakable, untamed, unconquerable."

II. Somewhere in England

My Father, John (1900-1990), was born to Dimitri and Joy Markessini in the capital city of Cephalonia, principal island of the Ionian Kingdom, a part of the Venetian Empire from 1197 through 1797, thence under British rule or influence until the end of World War I. Because of its seven islands, the Kingdom was known colloquially as the Epta Nisia and later, The United States of the Ionian Islands. Following the "Great War," confronting its heavy losses—in fact, the virtual loss of an entire generation—Great Britain renounced once and for all any and all claims to the former Venetian Ionian Kingdom having ceded it to Greece rather than Italy, effectively ending formal northern Italian influence in the Kingdom.

My paternal grandmother who was baptized with the English name Joy had an only sister (their maiden surname, Likouthi) who married an Englishman, a British Naval Officer. My Grand Aunt was said to be strikingly beautiful. She and her sister Joy were close and, as my Father put it, were "in and

7

out of each others' houses all the time." She bore two sons, Andrew (b. circa 1899) and Alexandre (b. circa 1901).

From the time they were toddlers, the two boys, Andrew and Alexandre, with their first cousin, my father, by birth year sandwiched in between, were inseparable and apparently by mutual consent spoke English with one another. My Grand Uncle understood the bond that had developed among the boys and generously saw to the schooling of all three so that they could remain companions together—his own sons and his nephew by marriage. They were entered and boarded at a British Public School on the Island of Corfu, the Ionian Academy (later and still named The Ionian University) established in 1824 by the Fifth Earl of Guilford, Frederick North, English Statesman and son of the then Prime Minister, for the sons, nephews, and younger brothers of the British Foreign Service and Military officers based in or near the Ionian Islands. At that time, the Island of Cephalonia was a naval base for the British in the Mediterranean. My father began his study of English law at the Academy and when home haunted the law courts of the Kingdom's capital city, which followed English law. (The boys could come home on weekends, a five-hour sail from Corfu.) I do not know the fields of study my two first cousins pursued at the Academy. If they did not graduate from the Academy, they were very close to doing so.

By all accounts, the two families lived prosperous, safe, and happy lives. My Grandparents owned three estates—A town house with a large fenced compound in the Capital City; a working farm of olive and citrus groves on the City outskirts, where my Grandmother, Joy, who oversaw the farm, also cultivated herbs, and roses, and jasmine from which she created perfumes for family and friends; and, a mansion retreat high in the redolent, pine-clad mountains surrounding the Markesinei clan village of Prokopata where their horses and English hounds were kept for hunting. It became John's haunt, a place to which he could ride his horse up from the farm and visit. There, with the guidance of their trainer, John was given the pick of a litter; named him Charon after the ferryman of Hades (But why, I can't imagine.); and spared him the harsh life of a hunting dog.

When Great Britain declared war against the Austro-Hungarian/German/ Turkish Alliance, the well-being of the two intertwined families took deathly turns. My uncle grew fearful for the lives of his two sons, still children, although many at that age were already being called into service, and sent his wife and sons by ship to his parents and their family Estate in England where they arrived safely. He remained behind to fight and, according to my father, was almost certainly killed in combat during the War. Father said that Uncle was the finest man he had ever known— handsome, tall, strong, courageous, kind, well-spoken but reserved to the point of silence when he needed to be, loyal to King and Country. If I know anything about my father, I know that he loved him.

My father tried and wanted to stay in the Kingdom in order to complete his studies and practice law. His father, a married Bishop and Abbot of Saint

Cathedral Interior, Monastery of Agios Gerasimos-Ionian Island of Cephalonia.

Gerasimos, the principal Cathedral and Monastery in the Kingdom, argued that in his view the only way he could keep his son out of military service was to have him enter Holy Orders. Something of a contest of wills ensued between him and his brother-in-law about what profession my father should engage, my Grand-Uncle fully believing that his nephew would make a gifted lawyer. Before John's birth, my Grandfather had chosen the Dean of the Theological Seminary in Athens to be Godfather to his son, and so he became. The stage had been set. But his son said No *to that choice of careers and left the Kingdom soon after his cousins. By that point, he had probably completed his schooling in pre-law.* *

Traveling alone, he landed safely in Liverpool, England, but was devastated by the poverty of the city and the impoverished condition of the country at that time and decided to attempt the United States. During the voyage on an Ionian ship owned by family friends sending their young men away from the War, he faced death. German U-boats kept the ship under constant fire and were torpedoing British civilian ships in the Atlantic. The ship was under duress, he said, and conditions aboard were bleak; he slept on a wooden board six inches thick. He landed safely and successfully in Norfolk, Virginia circa 1916 with identity papers in hand, in good health, and fluent in English.

Before landing and whilst the ship was still outward bound, he had tried to persuade a close friend and nephew of the ship owner to leave the ship with him whenever and wherever it docked in the United States. He believed

Sails Set, Boat Heads by the Lighthouse into Argostoli Harbor-Island of Cephalonia.

utterly that the ship would not survive the return trans-Atlantic voyage, but the young man said he could not abandon his uncle, even though he believed they would likely die. On its return voyage to the Ionian Islands, the ship was indeed torpedoed and sank with all lives lost.

When my father first told me of that misfortune, which he learned through family connections after he had landed; his eyes filled with tears, but he did not weep. He was no more than eighteen years of age, totally alone, emotionally battered, and physically exhausted. Somehow he survived and made his way to New York City where he found compatriots and eventually prospered.

At the time he arrived in America during the Great War—"The War to End All Wars," he must have understood that there could be no easy way back to his family, his home, and the privileged life he had known. His two first cousins, also still alive, both graduated Oxford University—I do not know what fields of study they pursued—and then fought in World War II where they were killed, according to my Father's surmise. In any case, my Father stopped this narrative of his family with his cousins' graduations from Oxford and subsequent military service, whether British Army or Navy, in keeping with their father' service, I do not know.

All of this was told me by my father. Because of his silence and sadness at narrative's end, I have always assumed that my Grand Aunt continued to live in England until her death and that my cousins were almost certainly killed in World War II. However, if they married before entering military service, they may have fathered children, now possibly adult men and women. I have always yearned to know of their existence wherever they may be.

So much for the devastation and unforeseen consequences of War.

<u>Note</u>: *The British Public School System graduates students with the equivalent of two years of college education in the United States. Most British public schools were and are highly selective on academic, financial, and social grounds. A family connection to the School is, and was, considered most desirable in admissions. At the Ionian University in Corfu, there are today three advanced curricula: pre-medicine, pre-law, and pre-Holy orders.

III. A Marriage

A love story: My parents met in New York City; it seems it was a love-at-first-sight experience for both of them. But as they were both rather private people, even their children, Jamie and I, had to make inferences, as closely as we could draw them.

Mother loved the City and visited as frequently as she could, staying with, or close to, two second cousins of hers, through the Govostes family line. She loved to go out dancing with "Teddy" (Theodore) because, as she put it, he was a marvelous dancer, especially waltzing and the tango. Teddy said he knew a fabulous guy and would she be interested in meeting him.

"Yes, why not?" That was Dad. She was twenty-two at the time; it was not long before he proposed, and she accepted, but her parents blocked the marriage.

In their view (and this could be unfair on my part), they had spent a great deal of money on grooming her for the marriage of their dreams and in the end she had thwarted them: Horseback riding (English style), education at an exclusive boarding school for young women to "finish" her*, painting and embroidering on silk, oil painting, music, French literature and language. Then they took her on the luxury liner, Saturnia, on a dream voyage, destination Athens and a coming out in Athenian Society. They were seeking a husband for her, a Greek aristocrat, preferably allied with the Greek Royal House, to confer upon them the final prestige of a title along with the wealth they had acquired. She was very pretty, refined, multilingual, American (It was 1931 and the Greeks sensed trouble ahead in Europe, so US citizenship could prove quite helpful.), and most of all rich—very attractive to the aristocrats with titles and education but little money.

She received six proposals of marriage, all of which she refused, and found the fierce running battles between the Monarchists and the Venezelists (who wanted to be rid of the German Royal House and Nobility) far more interesting to observe**. She did so from the rooftop gardens of the Hotel Acropolais near Syntagma Square where the small Vlahos family contingent sojourned in a luxury suite. There were machine-gun emplacements on the roofs of other buildings, which would engage in sporadic gunfire. My Grandfather, who was more sympathetic, I dare say, to her frustration than her mother, would climb onto the roof and haul her back down fearing for her life. When I asked her, Wasn't there even one young(ish) man who appealed to her among the six who

Aftermath, Wartime Street Fighting- Athens in Ruins, Greece.

had formally proposed? No, emphatically No, she said. After seeing and so-cializing with the tall, handsome, strong brothers, cousins, and uncles of the French and Irish Catholic young women who had been her classmates at Notre Dame Academy in Lowell,* she said she "couldn't abide" those "skinny, little shrimp-boats who thought they were something."

She and Dad corresponded regularly for six long years, and she escaped to New York City to visit with her cousins as often as she could. My Yiayia con-fided in me that she understood "exactly" what she was up to but never let on to Adamandia and knew my mother was meeting Dad secretly. I guess she had finally realized what an ordeal the marriage market in Athens had been for her daughter, who had become an American girl, albeit a cosmopolitan one. When Mother was twenty-eight, six years later, my Dad finally said Enough! He wanted her but had suffered enough rejection. The time was now or never. They married with the acquiescence of Mother's parents. His Italian cousin, Stephano, was his best man.

Diana's two cousins had a sister who visited Mother and Dad often in Man-hattan. By the time, Jamie and I were newly born, she herself was well along in her pregnancy with our soon-to-become cousin, her only daughter Marina. Marina met, fell in love with, and married a young man at the University of New Hampshire against initial parental resistance. Same story, he was outside the inner sanctum of the "Laconian Society," largely Americans of Spartan Greek heritage. What is more, he was Jewish. Both became successful lawyers.

But Marina was luckier than my Mother had been: Marina's mother knew what my Mother had suffered to marry Dad, "that Italian," *** so Marina's family was more compliant about her marriage. For a number of years, Marina and I relished each other's company in and around Alexandria, Virginia. That we both had married into Jewish families was an added bond. Just before Marina retired early and moved to her family home in Maine, we decided we had to see the Holocaust Museum together. We had concluded it was the only way we could bear it. Five hours later, we emerged into an afternoon full of sunlight virtually crawling on our hands and knees. It was devastating.

So much for the prejudices of this World magnified and cruelly executed a million-fold.

<u>Notes:</u> * The Sisters of Notre Dame de Namur, a Roman Catholic Institute, was founded in Amiens, France, in 1803 by Saint Julie Billiart (Countess of Gézaincourt) and Marie-Louise-Françoise Blin de Bourdon, also a French noblewoman. They and their postulant, Catherine Duchatel of Reims, made a vow to devote themselves to the Christian education of girls, further proposing to train religious teachers who would go wherever in the world their services were requested.

In August 1806, the first regular schools of the Sisters opened to a crush of students. The urgent need for Christian education among all classes of society in France at the time led the foundresses to modify their original plan of teaching only the poor and to open schools to all children, including those of the wealthy.

Nevertheless, in 1809, the insistent opposition of the local bishop to missions outside his diocese led to the moving of the Institute to Namur, Belgium (then under the auspices of Napoleon Bonaparte), from which the Institute eventually grew to become a worldwide organization on five continents.

In 1854, the Sisters of Notre Dame de Namur established L'Academie de Notre Dame de Namur in Lowell, Massachusetts, a boarding and finishing school for Catholic girls, under the Roman Catholic Archdiocese of Boston. At that time all of the teaching and administrative staffs were being imported from France and French-speaking Belgium. The Academy was attended by girls from French-speaking Canada and Latin America as well as from the United States. In the largely French-Catholic City of Lowell, the teaching, study, and use of French language and literature at the Academy were mandatory; study and practice of the arts were required.

**In 1928, then Prime Minister of Greece, Eleftherios Venizelos, staged a successful coup d'état and supported Greece as a Hellenic Republic. Greek society had been divided between the pro-Republican Venizelists and the Monarchists represented by the People's Party, who favored the ousted king, King George II, and refused to acknowledge the legitimacy of the Republic.

To this polarization was added the destabilizing involvement of the military in politics, which resulted in several coups and attempted coups, and an economy ruined by a decade of warfare and the influx of an estimated 1.5 million Greek refugees from Turkey. (Mother characterized the City of Athens as "inundated", with new sections of the City poorly built and "paved" in mud.)

Despite the efforts of Venizelos' reformist government, which remained in power until 1932, the worldwide Great Depression further undermined Greece's economy. The electoral victory of the so-called People's Party in 1933 and two failed Venizelist coups paved the way for the restoration of the reign of King George II from 1935 to 1947. Venizelos had feared the Germanic background of King George II, a descendant of the House of Glucksburg, and his strong economic and military ties to Germany, although by the start of World War II the King was believed to have developed pro-British feelings.

*** The resistance of the Peloponnesian Greeks against the Venetian Ionians is historic and well documented. In 1827, two years after liberation from the Ottoman Turks, the Greek National Assembly elected Count Giovanni Antonio Capo d'Istria (born on Corfu into an aristocratic Venetian family) the first President of a newly independent Greece. (Among other accomplishments, as a physician by profession, he introduced the first modern quarantine system in Greece, which brought epidemics of typhoid fever, cholera, and dysentery under control for the first time since the start of the War of Independence.) Yet, despite exemplary national service and an international reputation, Capo d'Istria's refusal to countenance the lawless tribalism of the Manni Peninsula near Sparta antagonized the Greek peasantry, leading to his brutal assassination in 1831 by chieftains of the Manni people, on the steps of the Church of Saint Spyridon in Nafplion.

IV. A Postscript

There remains the ordeal of my mother's father, John Vlahos. At age four-teen, he came alone to this country from Selasia, a small village near Sparta, Greece, not far from the somewhat less impoverished village into which his bride-to-be was born and raised. An only son, he was sent to America by a desperate widowed mother. When he arrived at Ellis Island in New York har-bor, immigration officers decided he had to be medically quarantined for a month to determine whether or not he was infected with tuberculosis. He was asymptomatic but nevertheless came from Mediterranean Europe where the disease was rampant. He lived alone there, isolated in a narrow room.

He found work, twelve hours a day from sunrise to sundown, in the textile mills of Lowell, Massachusetts and shared a room with a dozen boys and men, some of whom were indeed tubercular. They shared tea bags, he said; one bag traveled to infuse cup after cup.

*Men, Women, Children Labor in Textile Mills- Lancashire England,
Lawrence and Lowell, New England*

*He finally decided to escape. "We had to leave that place," he told me, "or it (their living and work conditions) would have killed us." ***

But he was the only one brave enough to go; some of those who stayed behind died young. They had mouths to feed in Europe.

He made a living by peddling produce from a pushcart. What saved him? Certainly, his innate strength, stamina, good looks, and fair coloring. And he was smart as the years proved. But he credited his very life to the Irish-American police on the beat who seemed to empathize with his plight and let him trade, alerting him to the moments when citations and round-ups of street peddlers were set to occur:

"Move along, John, you've got to move along now." (My Mother's clear voice in my mind's ear re-telling the tale.)

Some may well have had widowed mothers back home to whom they, too, were sending money.

Obviously, he remembered them—and their mercy; after all, he told me about that early time in his life—years after he had become a wealthy businessman. Good in 1926 for three-quarters of a million dollars on his signature alone. Through the long decade of our Great Depression, he did not once fail to make payroll—not by a dollar, not be a day. (So said my Mother who reviewed his books.)

He was the Grandfather I knew. He had courage, I dare say—and gratitude suffused his being.

<u>Note</u>: *Decades later, I learned my Grandfather's narrative of his perilous early life was substantially correct. Born in 1879, he worked in the Lowell textile mills at the turn of the twentieth century. By 1900, thanks to technological and competitive advances, textile employment demanded far more than in the City's early years. Working conditions for laborers in the mills, in particular the tolls extracted from their health and safety, had worsened. In every department of the mills, fewer workers tended more machinery than they had half a century earlier, and the machinery operated at much higher speeds. Moreover, in that year, in any one of Lowell's many textile factories, twelve to fourteen hours of exacting labor a day with half days on Saturday meant as much as 77 hours of work a week. In 1903, noted a knowledgeable observer, the New England mills commanded more work from their operatives than was common even in the mills of Great Britain.

Credits and Attributions

II. *Somewhere in England*

British Public Schools.

British Culture, British Customs and British Traditions: The British Education System England, Wales, Scotland, Northern Ireland. Primary, Secondary, Grammar Schools, Public Schools. Qualifications. The Learn English Network. (2020).

III. *A Marriage*

The Sisters of Notre Dame de Namur, a Roman Catholic Institute, Amiens, France and L'Academie de Notre Dame de Namur, Lowell, Massachusetts, United States of America.

Sisters of Notre Dame de Namur. Wikipedia, the Free Encyclopedia. (2020).

Count Giovanni Antonio Capo d'Istria, born Corfu, The Ionian Kingdom into an aristocratic Venetian family, first President of a newly independent Greece.
Capo d'Istria, Giovanni Antonio, Count. The Columbia Electronic Encyclopedia, 6th Ed. (2012). New York, New York: Columbia University Press.

Ioannis Kapodistrias. Wikipedia, the Free Encyclopedia. (2019).

Theros, The Honorable Patrick N., Greek Ambassador to the United States. *Kapodistrias: The Revolution's Greatest and Least Appreciated Hero.* (March 23, 2014). Washington, DC: Saint George Orthodox Church: The Hellenic Society Prometheus.

IV. A Postscript

The Lowell Textile Mills at the turn of the twentieth century.
Working Conditions. Lowell National Historical Park Handbook 140. (2015) Lowell, Massachusetts.

Illustrations – Credits and Attributions

I. *A Given Name*

Mid-wives Attend a Young Mother Giving Birth-Europe.

http:www.wikipedia.org. londonmidwifery_practice.org. Birthing in chair image via medinfo.ufl.edu

II. *Somewhere in England*

Cathedral Interior, Monastery of Agiost Gerasimos- Ionian Island of Cephalonia. Grandfather Archimandrite Demetrios Markessini, presided as Abbot. **Interior of Cathedral, Monastery of Agios Gerasimos, Island of Cephalonia, Greece.**

Berit (Photographer). File Photograph from Wikimedia Commons, license under the Creative Commons Attribution 2.0 Generic License <u>Wikipedia, The Free Encyclopedia.</u>

Retrieved from http:**www.wikimedia.org.**

II. *Somewhere in England*

Sails Set, Boat Heads by the Lighthouse into the Argostoli Harbor.- Island of Cephalonia Arriving from Corfu. Father's Weekly Trip from Public School **Fishing Boats in the Harbor. Early 20th Century Oil, circa 1915 from a collection of oil paintings for A. Burkhart, London, UK. Unsigned, Artist unknown. On board.**
Retrieved from **http:www. sulisfineart.com** and **https://i-pinimg.com/ originals**

III. *A Marriage*

Aftermath, Wartime Street Fighting- Athens in Ruins, Greece.
http: www.debate.org/Reference/ Greek Civil War

IV. *A Postscript*

Men, Women, Children Labor in Textile Mills- Lancashire England, A Model for the Textile Mills of Lawrence and Lowell, New England
McGrath, Jenna, with contributions by Denise Webb. London's Pulse Projects: Group Research Projects from students in HSCI 3423.

londonspulse.org/textile-workers

About the Author

JOAN MARKESSINI is the author of more than 100 publications, including books, documentary films, scientific articles in juried journals, articles in edited series, technical reports, and newspaper articles, among them *Perspectives on Leadership* in five volumes. Her writing has reached large audiences in scientific, technical, and educational fields as well as the general public. She has served her country as a Foreign Service officer, and has traveled in eighty-three countries and territories in five continents and two sub-continents on official business and for pleasure. She enjoys writing poetry and is founder and president of *WELLTrek International®, LLC.*